THE
ANSWERS

ABOUT THE AUTHOR

Neil Somerville has been interested in divination ever since he was a child, when he first discovered an old book on the psychic sciences belonging to his parents. Since then his interest and studies have led him to write many popular and best-selling books, including the annual and widely translated *Your Chinese Horoscope* series as well as *Chinese Success Signs* and *Chinese Love Signs*. He has also written for many magazines and newspapers.

A keen walker and traveller, Neil Somerville lives in Berkshire with his wife and two children.

THE
ANSWERS

NEIL SOMERVILLE

**BARNES
& NOBLE
BOOKS**

NEW YORK

This edition published by Barnes & Noble Publishing, Inc.
by arrangement with HarperElement
An Imprint of HarperCollins*Publishers*

2005 Barnes & Noble Books

M 10 9 8 7 6 5 4 3 2 1

ISBN 0 7607 7481 1

Printed and bound in Thailand by
Imago

THIS BOOK IS
DEDICATED TO

YOU

SOMETHING IS LEARNED EVERY TIME A BOOK IS OPENED.

CHINESE PROVERB

INTRODUCTION

The values of friendship are many but one important essence of a good friend is their readiness to offer support and advice. And, as you use this book, I hope that over time you will come to regard it as a friend, always there to give a few useful and helpful words.

To use the book is easy and it is based upon one of the oldest divinatory systems, that of divining by lines or picking a passage from a book at random and applying it to your situation. It is known that the ancient Greeks and Romans consulted the works of Homer and Virgil for divinatory purposes and since then many have used the Bible, the I Ching and dictionaries or drawn from books chosen by chance. However, often the randomly chosen lines can be difficult to interpret or apply to what is being asked.

The Answers has been written and compiled *specifically* for the purposes of divining by lines and throughout its pages are proverbs, maxims and advice that have been included for their value and insight. It makes this ancient divination system easier to do and understand.

In using this book, it is best to quieten your mind and think over the question, issue or situation you want to address. Keep your thoughts simple and clear. Then, with your question firmly in mind, close your eyes and open the book at random or flick through the pages until you feel ready to stop. When you have made your choice of page, open your eyes and discover the response given.

Read this carefully and reflect on its meaning and how the sentiments could apply to your question. Often this will give you helpful guidance. And even if the words do not quite tie in with what you had in mind, it will usually be possible to gauge whether the response is of a positive and encouraging nature or more cautionary. The key to using *The Answers* is to look for directions and indications.

If the answer given appears to bear no relation to your question, turn to another page at random and read this response. This may give a clearer answer but, as you read it, do not forget the original answer you received. In some ways the answers could be linked.

As with all divination systems, it is best not to repeat the same question within a short space of time. This way you will have more time to reflect on the answer you are given. However, do remember that the answer you receive is a guide and a guide only, and that in all your actions and decisions you are the master and arbiter.

I hope that as you consult this book – and divine by lines – the responses you receive will be of help and that over time you will come to regard *The Answers* as a personal friend, always there and willing to speak to you.

Use it well.

IT IS WISE TO SUBMIT TO DESTINY.

CHINESE PROVERB

Take your chance while you can.

USE YOUR STRENGTHS WELL.

DO NOT BE
DISCOURAGED.
ALLOW MORE
TIME.

ACT WHILE YOU HAVE REASON AND INCENTIVE.

NEVER TAKE ANYTHING FOR GRANTED.

BENJAMIN DISRAELI

Avoid hasty assumptions.

PROCEED QUIETLY
AND WITHOUT FUSS.
THE RESULT COULD
SURPRISE.

BE AN OPENER
OF DOORS.

RALPH WALDO EMERSON

Take the initiative.

A CHANGE IN
ATTITUDE COULD
CHANGE MUCH.

I NEVER HAD A POLICY. I HAVE JUST TRIED TO DO MY VERY BEST EACH AND EVERY DAY.

ABRAHAM LINCOLN

Much will now come from doing your best.

CONSIDER
ALTERNATIVES.
THERE COULD
BE BETTER
WAYS.

DILIGENCE LEADS TO RICHES.

CHINESE PROVERB

Use your talents well.

ADDRESS MISGIVINGS BEFORE THEY UNDERMINE MUCH.

IF
DISSATISFIED,
LOOK TO
CHANGE.

MUCH CAUTION DOES NO HARM.

PORTUGUESE PROVERB

Avoid unnecessary risks.

THINK AWHILE.
NEW THOUGHTS
COULD HELP.

Decide on your purpose *and act*.

HE WHO BRINGS IS WELCOME.

GERMAN PROVERB

Make a positive gesture.

DO NOT SHY
AWAY FROM
ACTION YOU
NEED TO TAKE.

NEVER DESPAIR, BUT IF YOU DO, WORK ON IN DESPAIR.

EDMUND BURKE

This is no time to give up.

INCREASE
YOUR
UNDERSTANDING.

GREAT THINGS ARE NOT DONE BY IMPULSE.

VINCENT VAN GOGH

Think plans through more carefully.

BE OPEN
TO OTHER
POSSIBILITIES.

PURPOSEFUL
EFFORT CAN LEAD
TO MUCH.

DREAM LOFTY DREAMS, AND AS YOU DREAM SO YOU BECOME.

JAMES ALLEN

Let your dreams and hopes encourage you on.

DO NOT SQUANDER
PRESENT CHANCES
OR IDEAS.

WISELY AND SLOW: THEY STUMBLE THAT RUN FAST.

WILLIAM SHAKESPEARE

Take more time.

CHANCE FAVOURS THE PREPARED MIND.

LOUIS PASTEUR

Prepare well and more will ultimately result.

WITHOUT A PURPOSE, NOTHING SHOULD BE DONE.

MARCUS AURELIUS

Be clear in your intent.

TRUST IN YOUR
ABILITIES.

LISTEN TO OTHERS. THERE IS AN IMPORTANT MESSAGE TO BE HEARD.

THEY CAN CONQUER WHO BELIEVE THEY CAN.

JOHN DRYDEN

Keep faith in what you are wanting.

Do what you can and is within your grasp.

KEEP YOUR
OPTIONS OPEN
A LITTLE
LONGER.

BE MORE
TRUSTING OF
YOURSELF AND
OTHERS.

WHEN FORTUNE KNOCKS, OPEN THE DOOR.

ITALIAN PROVERB

Take the chance while you can.

WITHOUT
COMMITMENT,
LITTLE WILL
RESULT.

THAT WHICH MUST BE WILL BE.

DANISH PROVERB

Accept situations so you can move forward.

PRESENT
SITUATIONS COULD
HAVE HIDDEN
BLESSINGS.
BE ALERT.

SEEK OUT THOSE WHO CAN HELP.

WHO DOES NOT TIRE ACHIEVES.

SPANISH PROVERB

Do not give up on your aims.

BE CAREFUL.
THIS IS NO
TIME FOR RISK
OR RUSH.

'No' is a good answer when given in time.

Danish proverb

If you have reservations, let these be known.

THE GREATER YOUR
RESOLVE, THE MORE
THAT CAN HAPPEN.

AVOID
DISTRACTION.
BE RESOLUTE
AND PURPOSEFUL.

HELP ANOTHER
AND IN SOME WAY
YOU TOO WILL
BE HELPED.

PRECAUTION IS BETTER THAN REPENTANCE.

GREEK PROVERB

Take greater care.

Avoid acting on impulse.

ACT BEFORE
CHANCES ARE
LOST.

PERSIST
PATIENTLY AND
YOU WILL
PREVAIL.

IF WAVERING
AND
DOUBTFUL,
RECONSIDER
YOUR PLANS.

BE RESOLVED AND THE THING IS DONE.

CHINESE PROVERB

Make a commitment and follow it through.

WITH THE GOOD WE BECOME GOOD.

DUTCH PROVERB

Join with those you admire.

ALLOW TIME.
THERE IS STILL
MUCH TO DO
AND UNDERSTAND.

CERTAIN
SITUATIONS
MAY COME
UNBIDDEN BUT
OFFER IMPORTANT
CHANCES.

DISAPPOINTMENTS
CAN OFTEN BE
THE START OF
SOMETHING NEW.

WHO WOULD WIN MUST LEARN TO BEAR.

GERMAN PROVERB

Overcome so you might gain.

KEEP FAITH —
NEW CHANCES
COULD SOON
ARISE.

In most undertakings problems *will* arise. It is worth persevering.

EXPECTATIONS
DO MUCH TO
GOVERN OUTCOMES.
KEEP THEM POSITIVE.

NEVER DESERT YOUR OWN LINE OF TALENT.

SYDNEY SMITH

Put your strengths to good use.

AVOID
COMPLACENCY.
GREATER
ATTENTION
CAN MAKE A
DIFFERENCE.

LET GO OF
UNHELPFUL
INFLUENCES.

THEY CAN ...
BECAUSE THEY
THINK THEY CAN.

Virgil

You can ... if you think you can.

LET IDEAS AND SITUATIONS TAKE SHAPE. THESE ARE WORTH GETTING RIGHT.

DO NOT LET
PRESENT CHANCES
OR EFFORTS GO
TO WASTE.

IT IS IMPOSSIBLE TO WIN THE GREAT PRIZES OF LIFE WITHOUT RUNNING RISKS.

THEODORE ROOSEVELT

Act and give yourself more chance.

APPRECIATE AND BUILD ON WHAT YOU HAVE.

NEW INITIATIVE
COULD MAKE A
DIFFERENCE.

BE UNDERSTANDING
OF OTHERS BUT
RESOLUTE IN YOUR
QUEST.

KEEP THINGS IN PERSPECTIVE.

ONE MUST HAVE THE COURAGE TO DARE.

FYODOR DOSTOEVSKY

To realize, be bold.

A SHORT REST IS ALWAYS GOOD.

DANISH PROVERB

A break could benefit.

THE WAY OF PROGRESS IS NEITHER SWIFT NOR EASY.

MARIE CURIE

It is worth greater determination.

PRIORITIZE
AND FOCUS ON
THE MOST
IMPORTANT.

Do not wait
for change.
Do what you
can now.

THE WILL IS EVERYTHING.

ITALIAN PROVERB

Be determined.

BELIEVE ONE WHO HAS TRIED IT.

VIRGIL

Seek out those with experience.

WITH GREATER CLARITY, MORE WILL HAPPEN.

BE TRUE TO
YOURSELF.
FOLLOW YOUR
INCLINATIONS.

TO SUCCEED,
MAKE SURE PRESENT
ACTIONS ARE IN
LINE WITH AIMS.

HE THAT NEVER FAILS NEVER GROWS RICH.

ITALIAN PROVERB

Do not let setbacks prevent another try.

BE CAUTIOUS,
LOOKING AT
THE REASONS
BEHIND ANY
DOUBTS.

TO ACCOMPLISH GREAT THINGS, WE MUST NOT ONLY ACT, BUT ALSO DREAM, NOT ONLY PLAN BUT ALSO BELIEVE.

ANATOLE FRANCE

With greater purpose more can result.

AVOID
DISTRACTION
ONTO LESSER
MATTERS.

CALM REFLECTION
AND DELIBERATION
WILL RESOLVE
MUCH.

ACT TO MAKE
IT HAPPEN.

DO NOT HANG UP ALL ON ONE NAIL.

GERMAN PROVERB

Take precautions.

RATHER LIGHT
A CANDLE
THAN COMPLAIN
ABOUT DARKNESS.

CHINESE PROVERB

Take constructive action.

BE DEFINITE IN
YOUR AIM.

NEVER REPENT A GOOD ACTION.

DANISH PROVERB

*Do what you feel is right
and helpful.*

CHANCE NEVER HELPS THOSE WHO DO NOT HELP THEMSELVES.

SOPHOCLES

Act and give yourself that chance.

LET YOUR HOOK
BE ALWAYS CAST;
IN THE POOL WHERE
YOU LEAST EXPECT
IT, THERE WILL BE
A FISH.

OVID

Be alert for opportunity.

PUT IDEAS TO THE TEST.

WHO DOES TOO MUCH OFTEN DOES LITTLE.

ITALIAN PROVERB

Be more focussed.

DO NOT
PREVARICATE.
BE FIRM IN
YOUR INTENT.

USE TALENTS
WELL. AIM FOR
THE BEST.

ACT UPON YOUR HUNCHES.

CHANGE YOURSELF AND FORTUNE WILL CHANGE.

PORTUGUESE PROVERB

Further your talents and more will become possible.

COURAGE AND PERSEVERANCE HAVE A MAGICAL TALISMAN.

JOHN QUINCY ADAMS

*Keep faith in what you are doing and *wanting*.*

DO NOT BE DRAWN
INTO UNHELPFUL
SITUATIONS. STAND
YOUR GROUND.

KEEP YOUR WITS ABOUT YOU.

Avoid taking too much for granted. Put in the effort.

CONCENTRATE ON
WHAT YOU *CAN* DO
RATHER THAN WHAT
YOU CANNOT.

IN THE LONG RUN MEN HIT ONLY WHAT THEY AIM AT.

HENRY DAVID THOREAU

Be clear in your aims.

HOLD BACK.
THERE IS MORE
TO CONSIDER.

TOO MUCH HASTE
COULD LEAD
TO MISTAKES.
BE CAREFUL.

BASE YOUR
DECISION ON
KNOWN FACTS.

THE SECRET OF GETTING AHEAD IS GETTING STARTED.

MARK TWAIN

Make a positive start.

GOOD IS THE DELAY WHICH MAKES SURE.

PORTUGUESE PROVERB

Check the situation more fully.

AVOID
DIVERTING
FROM YOUR
TRUE AIM.

DO NOT BE
RETICENT WHEN
MUCH COULD BE
GAINED.

BETTER ASK THAN GO ASTRAY.

ITALIAN PROVERB

Ask those with experience to help.

BY DOING,
IMPORTANT
DOORS WILL
OPEN.

GOOD THINGS REQUIRE TIME.

DUTCH PROVERB

Be patient. It will be worth the wait and commitment.

Do not be held
back by reversals.
Try again — wiser
and better
prepared.

DO SOMETHING RATHER THAN NOTHING.

GREATER
MODERATION
COULD ULTIMATELY
LEAD TO MORE.

BE WHAT NATURE INTENDED YOU FOR, AND YOU WILL SUCCEED.

SYDNEY SMITH

Do what you do best.

AVOID CHANGE
FOR THE SAKE
OF CHANGE.

Be definite.
Hesitancy now
could undermine
much.

LEARN FROM WAYS
THAT HAVE WORKED
FOR OTHERS; THEY
TOO COULD WORK
FOR YOU.

EVERY ACTION YOU
TAKE IS, IN SOME
WAY, IMPORTANT.
ACT WISELY.

OPPORTUNITIES DO NOT WAIT.

GREEK PROVERB

Make much of present chances.

IF NOT YOU, THEN WHO?

IF NOT NOW, THEN WHEN?

HILLEL

Take responsibility.

DEVELOPMENT
NOW CAN LEAD TO
FUTURE GAIN.

SIMPLIFY, SIMPLIFY AND YOU WILL BEGIN TO MAKE FAR GREATER HEADWAY.

HENRY DAVID THOREAU

Decide and concentrate on your priorities.

LOOK CLOSELY
AT MISGIVINGS.
THEY WILL
TELL MUCH.

SELF DONE, WELL DONE.

GERMAN PROVERB

It rests with you to do. And do well.

TURN
INTENTION TO
ACTION.

LET THE GLORY
OF YOUR AIMS
ENCOURAGE
YOU ON.

THERE IS A GREAT DIFFERENCE BETWEEN SAID AND DONE.

PUERTO RICAN PROVERB

Act and so move your hopes and situation forward.

FORTUNE IS EVER SEEN ACCOMPANYING INDUSTRY.

OLIVER GOLDSMITH

Work determinedly towards what you want.

SHOW YOU CARE.
IT *WILL* MAKE A
DIFFERENCE.

EITHER DO NOT ATTEMPT AT ALL, OR GO THROUGH WITH IT.

OVID

Decide now and so end the uncertainty.

ALL COMES RIGHT TO HIM WHO CAN WAIT.

FRENCH PROVERB

Allow time for efforts to take effect.

WHAT YOU DO
NOW CAN MAKE
A DIFFERENCE.
ACT WELL.

LOOK TO DEVELOP SO YOU CAN BETTER ADVANCE.

CONSIDERABLE
effort may be
required. It rests
with you.

LISTEN WELL TO
LOVED ONES.

FROM LITTLE THINGS MEN GO ON TO GREAT.

DUTCH PROVERB

Nurture hopes so they may develop and grow.

IN TIMES OF STRESS, BE BOLD AND VALIANT

HORACE

Draw on strengths that lie within you.

CONSIDER YOUR
REASONS MORE
CAREFULLY.

TO PROGRESS, GET FURTHER SUPPORT.

IMAGINE THE
DESIRED OUTCOME
AND LET THIS
IMAGE ENCOURAGE
YOU ON.

DON'T PROMISE WHAT YOU CANNOT PERFORM.

TURKISH PROVERB

Be realistic in what you set yourself to do.

ALL THINGS ARE DIFFICULT BEFORE THEY ARE EASY.

THOMAS FULLER

It is worth the effort to reap the benefits.

DO WHAT YOU CAN, WITH WHAT YOU HAVE, WHERE YOU ARE.

THEODORE ROOSEVELT

Act well upon present chances.

DO NOT DO TOO
MUCH SINGLE-
HANDED. SEEK
ADVICE AND HELP.

BE WARY OF
UNHELPFUL
INFLUENCES.
THEY COULD
UNDERMINE MUCH.

READ AND REAP THE REWARDS.

CHINESE PROVERB

To advance, look to develop.

BELIEVE AND
ACT UPON YOUR
AIMS. NOW IS
THE TIME.

TAKE HEART.
THE SEEDS OF
SUCCESS ARE OFTEN
BORN THROUGH
DIFFICULTY.

CONSTANT EFFORT YIELDS CERTAIN SUCCESS.

It is *worth persisting.*

DO NOT WASTE
TIME ON THAT
WHICH IS NOT
HELPFUL.

AVOID OVER-
REACTION. CAREFUL
DELIBERATION
WILL HELP.

A RESOLUTE MANNER CARES NOTHING ABOUT DIFFICULTIES.

TAMIL PROVERB

Remain steadfast. It will be worth the effort.

TAKE CONCERTED
ACTION. NOTHING
WILL HAPPEN
OTHERWISE.

GOOD COUNSEL BRINGS GOOD FRUIT.

GERMAN PROVERB

Seek out those with the knowledge to help.

RIGHT THOUGHTS AND RIGHT EFFORTS WILL INEVITABLY BRING THE RIGHT RESULTS.

JAMES ALLEN

Act rightly. And justly.

WHO OFTEN CHANGES, SUFFERS.

―――

FRENCH PROVERB

Be more persevering.

PLOUGH DEEP AND YOU WILL HAVE PLENTY OF CORN.

SPANISH PROVERB

Prepare yourself well.

FACE THE
CHALLENGE AND
DISCOVER NEW
STRENGTHS.

YOUR DREAMS
ARE OFTEN GOALS
WAITING TO
HAPPEN. BUT
THEY NEED
ACTING UPON.

RESOLVE, AND THOU ART FREE.

HENRY WADSWORTH LONGFELLOW

*Make a firm decision and rid
yourself of current uncertainties.*

DO WHATEVER
IS MOST HELPFUL.
BUT YOU MUST *DO*.

GREAT RESULTS CANNOT BE ACHIEVED AT ONCE.

SAMUEL SMILES

Be patient and persevering.

BE WARY OF
FALSEHOOD.

DEVELOP AND
NEW DOORS
WILL OPEN UP.

CLARIFY YOUR AIMS
AND END THE
UNCERTAINTY.

THOSE THINGS THAT HURT, INSTRUCT.

BENJAMIN FRANKLIN

Challenging situations can *ultimately lead to much.*

CONCENTRATE ON ONE THING AT A TIME.

DO NOT DELAY
WHAT YOU CAN
DO NOW.

HE THAT IS AFRAID TO SHAKE THE DICE WILL NEVER THROW A SIX.

CHINESE PROVERB

Take the chance while you can.

GIVE WELL
OF YOURSELF,
REMAINING
DETERMINED IN
YOUR QUEST.

GREAT THOUGHTS ALWAYS COME FROM THE HEART.

VAUVENARGUES

Listen to your feelings. These are the voice of the real you.

SOW MUCH, REAP MUCH; SOW LITTLE, REAP LITTLE.

To gain, you have to make the effort.

DO NOT TRY
FOR SOMETHING
YOU ARE NOT
READY FOR.

GO AND WAKE UP YOUR LUCK.

PERSIAN PROVERB

Take some positive action.

IT DOES NOT MATTER HOW SLOWLY YOU GO, SO LONG AS YOU DO NOT STOP.

CONFUCIUS

Proceed at your own pace, but determinedly.

DO NOT FORCE
SITUATIONS
UNNECESSARILY.
WAIT AND WATCH.

ACT UPON YOUR
AIMS. THIS IS NO
TIME FOR DELAY OR
EXCUSE.

VARIOUS ARE THE ROADS TO FAME.

ITALIAN PROVERB

*Do not feel restricted to one course
when others too could benefit.*

ATTEND
CAREFULLY TO
THE DETAILS.

IT IS NEVER TOO LATE TO BE WHAT YOU MIGHT HAVE BEEN.

GEORGE ELIOT

Do not give up on your aims.

ENOUGH IS GREAT RICHES.

DANISH PROVERB

Be careful not to over-extend yourself.

IMPROVE
YOURSELF SO
THAT YOU MAY
FLOURISH.

IN MATTERS OF DOUBT, BOLDNESS IS OF THE GREATEST VALUE.

PUBLILIUS SYRUS

End the uncertainty and act.

DRAW BACK
AWHILE,
REFLECTING
ON WHAT IS BEST
FOR YOU.

WE CANNOT DO EVERYTHING AT ONCE, BUT WE CAN DO SOMETHING AT ONCE.

CALVIN COOLIDGE

Do what you can do now.

YOUR OWN RESOLUTION TO SUCCESS IS MORE IMPORTANT THAN ANY OTHER ONE THING.

ABRAHAM LINCOLN

Believe more fully in yourself and aims. You really *can do much.*

WHEN THERE IS NO FISH IN ONE SPOT CAST YOUR NET IN ANOTHER.

CHINESE PROVERB

Try other possibilities.

Avoid rush.
There is more to
be considered.

A NOBODY TODAY, A PRINCE TOMORROW.

LATIN PROVERB

*Do not give up. Changes in fortune
can be dramatic and swift.*

ADOPT THE PACE OF NATURE: HER SECRET IS PATIENCE.

RALPH WALDO EMERSON

Give what you want more time.

GIVE YOUR DREAMS
ALL YOU'VE GOT
AND YOU'LL BE
AMAZED AT THE
ENERGY THAT
COMES OUT OF YOU.

WILLIAM JAMES

THE PERSON WHO SAYS IT CANNOT BE DONE SHOULD NOT INTERRUPT THE PERSON DOING IT.

CHINESE PROVERB

Do not underestimate what is possible.

IF YOUR DESIRE
IS GENUINE,
YOUR EFFORTS
CAN LEAD TO
MUCH.

AFTER A BAD HARVEST SOW AGAIN.

LATIN PROVERB

Do not let disappointments prevent other attempts.

SET YOUR SAIL ACCORDING TO THE WIND.

FRENCH PROVERB

Show greater flexibility.

AVOID MAKING
THE SITUATION
WHAT IT IS NOT.

PAUSE AWHILE.
REFRESHED YOU
WILL BE MORE
EFFECTIVE.

FORGIVE AND FORGET.

GERMAN PROVERB

Move away from the unhelpful.

KEEP
DEVELOPING
AND MORE
WILL OPEN UP
TO YOU.

CHANGE IS
INEVITABLE
BUT WITH IT
COMES NEW
POSSIBILITY.

AVOID COMMITMENT TO SOMETHING YOU MAY BE UNCOMFORTABLE WITH.

AS IS OUR CONFIDENCE, SO IS OUR ABILITY.

WILLIAM HAZLITT

Believe. You have it within you to do much.

Do not go against your better judgement.

BE POSITIVE.
YOU HAVE MUCH
TO OFFER.

ALLOW TIME
FOR EVENTS TO
UNFOLD.

WE ARE WHAT WE REPEATEDLY DO.

ARISTOTLE

*Make sure current actions are in
line with your aims.*

CHECK SITUATIONS MORE THOROUGHLY.

Rely on
yourself.

JEAN DE LA FONTAINE

The responsibility lies with you.

PERSEVERANCE BRINGS SUCCESS.

DUTCH PROVERB

Remain committed in your quest.

WITHOUT STRONG
ENOUGH REASON,
RESULTS COULD
DISAPPOINT.

OUR PLANS MISCARRY BECAUSE THEY HAVE NO AIM.

SENECA

To progress, be clear in objective and intent.

ALL COMES RIGHT TO HIM WHO CAN WAIT.

FRENCH PROVERB

Show patience and allow time for efforts to take effect.

Do not hold back
from what you
can do. Take
control.

AVOID WISHFUL
THINKING. DEAL
WITH SITUATIONS
AS THEY ARE.

LIFE IS LARGELY A MATTER OF EXPECTATION.

HORACE

Believe in yourself for you are truly capable of much.

BUILD WELL
ON PRESENT
SITUATIONS.

AVOID HASTE.
CONSIDER THE
CONSEQUENCES
MORE CAREFULLY.

WHAT YOU HAVE TO DO, DO WITHOUT DELAY.

CHINESE PROVERB

Seize the moment and chance.

WHO CHANGES HIS CONDITION CHANGES FORTUNE.

ITALIAN PROVERB

*Adapt and develop and so give
yourself more chance.*

ACT DETERMINEDLY
AND BE HELD BACK
NO LONGER.

LITTLE BY LITTLE ONE GOES FAR.

SPANISH PROVERB

Progress steadily, one step at a time.

FAILURE IS THE FOUNDATION OF SUCCESS, AND THE MEANS BY WHICH IT IS ACHIEVED.

LAO-TZU

Learn well from reversals and in time you will *profit.*

WATCH AND
LISTEN. THERE
IS STILL MUCH
TO CONSIDER.

HE THAT SOWS WELL REAPS WELL.

SPANISH PROVERB

Prepare well for what you have in mind.

BE YOURSELF
AND LET YOUR
TRUE TALENTS
EMERGE.

PLODDING WINS THE RACE.

AESOP

Keep going.

ACT FOR THE GOOD
OF OTHERS AND, IN
SOME WAY, YOU TOO
WILL BENEFIT.

HESITATE NO
LONGER.

ENERGY AND PERSISTENCE CONQUER ALL THINGS.

BENJAMIN FRANKLIN

Keep striving. Persistence will be rewarded.

AS FORTUNE IS SOUGHT SO IT IS FOUND.

GERMAN PROVERB

Give yourself more chance.

MUCH DEPENDS ON YOUR WILLINGNESS.

BETTER TO DO NOTHING THAN TO DO ILL.

PLINY

If you have uncertainties, wait.

TAKE GREATER CONTROL.

THINK OF THE
CONSEQUENCES
IF YOU DID
NOTHING.

MANY THINGS ARE LOST FOR WANT OF ASKING.

ENGLISH PROVERB

Be prepared to ask.

SUIT YOURSELF TO THE TIMES.

GERMAN PROVERB

Be flexible in approach.

Avoid assuming too much too soon.

IF PRESENT ACTIONS
DISAPPOINT, TRY
ANOTHER WAY.

WE DO IN HASTE AND REPENT AT LEISURE.

GERMAN PROVERB

Avoid rash action.

YOUR HOPES AND
IDEAS ARE LIKE
GEMS, WORTH
POLISHING AND
PERFECTING.

ACT HONESTLY AND BOLDLY.

DANISH PROVERB

*Go forward, knowing much
is possible.*

THE ROAD TO
SUCCESS CAN
BE ARDUOUS BUT
ITS JOURNEY
WORTHWHILE.
IT *IS* WORTH
PRESSING ON.

YOU CANNOT DO
EVERYTHING. DEAL
WITH THE MOST
IMPORTANT.

WHAT HAVE YOU
TO LOSE BY NOT
ACTING? IF LITTLE,
GO AHEAD.

TO PROGRESS,
APPLY YOURSELF
MORE FULLY TO
THE MATTER.

DO NOT UNDERESTIMATE WHAT YOU CAN DO.

DELAY ALWAYS BREEDS DANGER.

MIGUEL DE CERVANTES

Do not let present chances slip.

LET FEELINGS
OF DISCONTENT
ENCOURAGE YOU TO
BETTER THINGS.

VICTORY BELONGS TO THE MOST PERSEVERING.

NAPOLEON BONAPARTE

Do not let up in your present efforts.

STICK TO WAYS
THAT WORK
BEST FOR YOU.

BE BOLD AND LET
YOUR VOICE AND
TALENTS PREVAIL.

DO NOT LET
SITUATIONS DRIFT.
DECIDE THEN ACT.

WHAT IS LONG SPOKEN OF HAPPENS AT LAST.

DUTCH PROVERB

Your efforts could soon be rewarded.

DO NOT SHY AWAY
FROM CHANGE
WHEN MUCH CAN
BE GAINED.

HEAR BOTH SIDES.

LATIN PROVERB

*Be aware of what others may say
or advise.*

Do not be
left wondering,
'what if?'
Find out.

EVERYTHING HAS ITS TIME.

PORTUGUESE PROVERB

Be patient and persevering.

BE HOPEFUL.
YOU HAVE GREAT
STRENGTHS TO
DRAW UPON.

WHAT APPEAR TO BE CALAMITIES ARE OFTEN THE SOURCES OF FORTUNE.

BENJAMIN DISRAELI

Difficulties can often set you on a better track.

AFTER RAIN COMES SUNSHINE.

FRENCH PROVERB

Be optimistic.

GREATER
FLEXIBILITY WILL
LEAD TO MORE.

REFLECT QUIETLY
AND MORE WILL
BECOME CLEAR.

Do not be
resistant to
change. Use it
to discover
and grow.

HE THAT SEEKS FINDS.

SPANISH PROVERB

Act well upon your aims.

VISUALIZE YOUR
GOAL AND LET
THIS IMAGE GUIDE
YOU FORWARD.

MISFORTUNE OFTEN SHARPENS THE GENIUS.

OVID

*Let present difficulties be the
catalyst for new ideas.*

A SHORT CUT IS OFTEN A WRONG CUT.

DANISH PROVERB

Be thorough.

RISE TO THE
CHALLENGE. SHOW
YOUR WORTH.

AVOID HASTE.
ALLOW MORE TIME
TO THINK MATTERS
THROUGH.

FORTUNE IS USUALLY ON THE SIDE OF THE INDUSTRIOUS.

SAMUEL SMILES

Work hard and well.

MAKE MORE OF
YOUR EXPERIENCE.
THIS IS WORTH
MUCH.

THE MIDDLE PATH IS THE SAFE PATH.

GERMAN PROVERB

Stick to what you know and feels right.

BRING DOUBTS
INTO THE OPEN
SO THEY CAN
BE ADDRESSED.

DO NOT DOUBT
YOUR ABILITIES.
USED WELL THESE
CAN BRING GREAT
PROFIT.

THERE IS NO FAILURE EXCEPT IN NO LONGER TRYING.

ELBERT HUBBARD

Do not relax present efforts.

BE MORE OPEN
WITH FEELINGS
AND AIMS.

AN OAK IS NOT FELLED AT ONE BLOW.

SPANISH PROVERB

*Keep trying until you get the
results you desire.*

WHAT YOU DO, DO THOROUGHLY.

FRENCH PROVERB

Extra attention can *make a difference.*